1996

100 Paintings from the Boston Museum

100 Paintings from the Boston Museum

Museum of Fine Arts, Boston

Distributed by New York Graphic Society · Greenwich, Connecticut

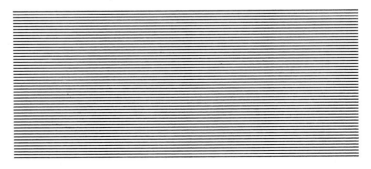

Published 1970 by Museum of Fine Arts, Boston
Library of Congress Catalogue Card Number: 70-101357
Printed in Western Germany by Brüder Hartmann, West Berlin
Designed by Carl F. Zahn

The one hundred paintings published here comprise the exhibition at
The Metropolitan Museum of Art, May 29 to July 26, 1970.

Notes on the paintings by Kent Sobotik

Introduction

Museum collections are usually narratives writ large in the script of a strong personality, or group of such personalities acting together. This is particularly true of the Asiatic, Classical, Egyptian, and Textile collections in the Boston Museum. But no individuals dominate the history of the Department of Paintings. Nor do the merchant princes who enriched the public collections in New York, Chicago, and Cleveland. Rather, the collection has grown from the artistic heritage of Boston itself; the continuing generosity of a host of private collectors; the single forays of a particular and enthusiastic trustee, director, or curator; and the essential ingredient that must supplement the administration of any well-run museum—luck. The collection of paintings, one of the oldest in America, has been in the process of formation for one hundred years. It therefore reflects with singular accuracy the changing tastes of American society, and the individualism of Bostonians.

When the first Museum building opened on July 4, 1876, a brilliant array of American paintings was permanently deposited by the Boston Athenaeum and the City of Boston—portraits by Copley, Stuart, and Neagle; historical works by Trumbull and West, among others. In due course the Museum's Copleys swelled to a total of some sixty, almost every one of which came to the Museum from family pride and tradition. Some, such as the portrait of Paul Revere (72), came from heirs of the sitter; others, such as the portrait of Mrs. Skinner (73), came from the artist's descendants. A similar number of Stuarts came by virtue of the same impulse.

Even before the first museum building was designed, the trustees had begun to collect. The first registered acquisition, a gift in 1870, was an American painting, *Elijah in the Desert* (77) by Washington Allston. The early trustees also responded to contemporary American artists, especially those with New England associations. In 1899 they bought Winslow Homer's *The Lookout—"All's Well"* (83), a classic that achieves as high a synthesis of color, form, and symbol as Homer ever reached in his painting. John Singer Sargent, admired and patronized in Boston throughout his career, is represented here by *The Daughters of Edward Darley Boit* (82), a work of striking design and originality inspired by Sargent's idol, Velázquez.

Later in the Museum's history, the M. and M. Karolik collection of American painting, 1800–1865, brought the Museum a rare representation of a largely neglected field of American art. Maxim Karolik, the Russian emigré, by his vivid personality and persuasive ways first rescued this field from "un-appreciation." It has since become a veritable racecourse of competition between museums and private collectors. Among the three hundred works in the Karolik collection are paintings by Fitz Hugh Lane, Heade (81), and Peto (88) and surprising group portraits by Erastus Salisbury Field and Henry F. Darby (78).

The first acquisition of the Museum in its first year was an American painting; prophetically, in the second year, the trustees welcomed the gift of two great French paintings, François Boucher's *The Halt at the Spring* (40) and *The Return from Market* (41). Thus the two main streams of the collection—American and European—were established at the very start, and Bostonians continued to collect and appreciate art of all kinds far removed from their own Yankee environment. When Courbet's realistic hunting subject *The Quarry* (44), was first shown in Boston, for example, it was bought by the Allston Club, a band of artists led by William Morris Hunt. Hunt was one of their own, and Bostonians listened to him. He had studied in Paris as a young man, and through a devoted friendship with Millet came to know and champion the Barbizon School, indeed introducing such painters as Millet, Corot, and Courbet to Boston and America. Every Bostonian had to have his Millet, and Quincy Adams Shaw left over sixty of them which came to the Museum in 1917. Boston now had the largest Millet collection extant.

For Bostonians it was only a short step from Barbizon realism to that other marvelous invention of the French—Impressionism. Again a Boston painter pioneered, but this time a lady: Lilla Cabot Perry. Mrs. Perry spent ten summers in Monet's village of Giverny in order to learn directly from the artist. She bought his work and encouraged her friends at home to do the same. Hence the dealer Durand-Ruel's annual visits to Boston in the late eighties. Hence the Boston Museum's thirty-five Monets, ranging from 1867 to 1908, and all but two of them given by Boston collectors. The other Impressionists were equally admired, and almost as generously given: six Sisleys, eight Pissarros, nineteen Renoirs and twelve Degas. Mrs.

J. Montgomery Sears, who was Mrs. Jack Gardner's only rival as a Back Bay figure, collected under the guidance of Mary Cassatt, and left the Museum Manet's *The Street Singer* (53). Another great collector, Robert Treat Paine 2nd, in 1935 gave the first of five van Goghs now in the Museum, the universally loved *The Postman Roulin* (64). His munificent gifts and bequests include *Madame Cézanne in a Red Armchair* (62) and Degas' *Duke and Duchess of Morbilli* (51). John T. Spaulding left the fruits of his independent and energetic collecting to the Museum in 1948. He gave the Painting Department alone over ninety works, by European artists such as Cézanne, van Gogh, Manet, Sisley, Redon, and Renoir and by Americans such as Henri, Bellows, and Hopper.

The trustees of this period matched wits and purchases with private collectors. They bought Degas' *Carriage at the Races* (52), which was in the first Impressionist exhibition of 1874, and boldly ignoring the Depression bought not only what is perhaps the most beloved Renoir in America, *Le Bal à Bougival* (60), but also Gauguin's monumental *D'où venons-nous? Que sommes-nous? Où allons-nous?* (67), which compares with Seurat's *Dimanche à la Grande Jatte* as one of the most original works of the nineteenth century.

Nineteenth-century Bostonians were fascinated with France. They were inspired to build America's first boulevard, Back Bay's Commonwealth Avenue, and line it with houses in the style of the French Second Empire. Yet they did not neglect the old masters. Henry Lee Higginson, founder of the Boston Symphony Orchestra, led the way by his purchase in 1889 of Rogier van der Weyden's *St. Luke Painting the Virgin* (7), the first great Flemish picture to come to America. Latter-day trustees followed Higginson's example when in 1963 they acquired a brilliantly preserved anonymous masterwork of fifteenth-century Flanders, *The Martyrdom of St. Hippolytus* (8).

Italian works of all schools have claimed Boston loyalties. The impetus came first from Boston's James Jackson Jarves and his Italian "primitives" once castigated by a journalist as "pre-Giottesque ligneous daubs," and then from the imperious collecting of Mrs. Jack Gardner and the influence of her mentor, Bernard Berenson. Today the collection includes works by Duccio (1), Barna da Siena (3), and Giovanni di Paolo (10), and is carried forward in time by a representation of the Venetian school of Titian (15), Tintoretto (16), Guardi (21), Canaletto (20), and Tiepolo (42). A recent addition (1958) to the Italian collection is Il Rosso Fiorentino's *The Dead*

Christ with Angels (17). Long considered a lost work, it must now rank as the most distinguished Italian Mannerist work in America.

Boston is—and with cause—proud of its pioneering tastes. Just as Henry Lee Higginson brought the first great Flemish painting to America, other Boston donors and trustees introduced America to the first museum-owned Chardin, the first Millet, the first Degas, the first Monet, and also the first El Greco. As early as 1903, spurred on by a letter written from Spain to the Director by John Singer Sargent, the trustees bought El Greco's fluid, nervous, personal portrait of *Fray Felix Hortensio Paravicino* (22). Quite possibly Sargent also played a role three years earlier in the Museum's purchase of Veláz-quez' *Don Baltasar Carlos and His Dwarf* (23).

The opulent *Don Carlos* and the austere *Fray Felix* are but two punctuation marks in the artistic history of the seventeenth century —an incomparable age for painting in Western Europe. In Holland, the art rose to new heights. The Museum has recently acquired fur-ther examples of two of those aspects of painting in which the Dutch excelled—landscape and portraiture. Jacob van Ruisdael's *A Rough Sea* (29) is a late work of awesome beauty. Rembrandt's companion portraits of Rev. Johannes Elison and his wife (26 and 27) are su-preme, flawlessly preserved examples of his early work.

Obviously seventeenth-century Dutch art appeals to Bostonians as it appealed to the burghers of Amsterdam. Perhaps they see their own Yankee history reflected in the staunch and God-fearing like-nesses of Elison and his wife. Bostonians cherish history, using it thriftily to inform the present and chart the future. This impulse has brought to Boston a long memory of painting—not only the hieratic images of Christ and the Apostles from a twelfth-century monastery in Catalonia, the earliest paintings in the collection, but also the more extravagant images of our own time: the thunderous denunciation of war in Picasso's *Rape of the Sabines* (97), the chromatic dynamism of Nicholas de Staël's *Rue Gauguet* (98), the lyrical vision of Lee Gatch's *Gothic Night* (99), and the spontaneity of Franz Kline's *Probst I* (100).

The next hundred years will present their own opportunities and challenges. These will be met with the confidence born of a first century well-spent in the Boston manner. It is a manner that is both quietly productive and steadfastly dependable—as the painting col-lection of the Boston Museum surely demonstrates.

PERRY T. RATHBONE, *Director*, Museum of Fine Arts, Boston

Catalogue

I

DUCCIO DI BUONINSEGNA, Sienese, ca. 1255–1319
Triptych of the Crucifixion with St. Nicholas and St. Gregory
Tempera on panel, 24 × 31 in. overall
Grant Walker and Charles Potter Kling Funds 45.880

This panel is the only work by Duccio in the United States that is not part of his *Maestà* altarpiece for the cathedral of Siena. Simone Martini (1285–1344) has been suggested as the author of the wings, which are surely by a separate hand. The painted back of the panel simulates intarsia and resembles the painted back of the Madonna and Child by Duccio in the National Gallery, London.

Former Collections: William Young Ottley; John Pierpont Morgan, Sr., Wall Hall, Aldenham, Hertfordshire.
References: G. H. Edgell, "An Important Triptych of the Sienese Trecento," MFA *Bulletin* 44, no. 256 (June 1946), pp. 33–41; —, "A Crucifixion by Duccio with Wings by Simone Martini," *Burlington Magazine* 88 (May 1946), pp. 107–12; Renée Arb, "A Reappraisal of the Boston Museum's Duccio," *Art Bulletin* 41, no. 2 (June 1959), pp. 191–98.

2

BARNABA DA MODENA, Modenese, active 1362–1383
Virgin and Child
Tempera on panel, 39¹/₈ × 25 in.
Gift of Mrs. Walter Scott Fitz 15.951

Basically Byzantine in style, but with a suggestion of Giotto's new humanity, this panel by Barnaba probably dates from 1365–70.

Former Collection: R. Langton Douglas, London.
Reference: Wadsworth Athenaeum, *An Exhibition of Italian Panels and Manuscripts from the Thirteenth and Fourteenth Centuries in Honor of Richard Offner* (Hartford, 1965), pp. 18–19, no. 13.

3

BARNA DA SIENA, Sienese, active ca. 1350
The Marriage of St. Catherine
Tempera on panel, 53 × 42¹/₈ in.
Sarah Wyman Whitman Fund 15.1145

This painting by one of the few outstanding painters active in Siena after the Black Death possesses a rare iconographical feature. The saint is married to the adult Christ, not the infant Christ in the arms of the Virgin. Two knights shielded by an archangel have thrown down their arms and are embracing. The theme of victory over violence is buttressed by scenes of St. Margaret and St. Michael subduing demons. Evidently the painting was a votive offering to commemorate the reconcilation of a feud.

Former Collection: Alexander Barker, London.
References: G. H. Edgell, *A History of Sienese Painting* (New York, 1932), p. 163; Millard Meiss, *Painting in Florence and Siena after the Black Death* (Princeton, 1951), pp. 110 ff.

2

3

4

4

SANO DI PIETRO, Sienese, 1406–1481
Virgin and Child with Angels
Tempera on panel, 22^{1}/$_{2}$ × 15^{1}/$_{4}$ in.
Bequest of Caroline Isabella Wilby 97.229

5

Death of the Virgin
Bohemian, 14th century
Tempera on panel, 39 × 27^{3}/$_{4}$ in.
William F. Warden Fund 50.2716

A work of the international court of the Emperor Charles IV in
Prague, the panel shows the assimilation and transformation of ele-
ments from Italian, French, and Austrian art. It is closely related
to the masterpiece of the period, the Vyšší Brod (Hohenfurt) Altarpiece in the National Gallery, Prague (ca. 1350–60). The cleric
(donor?) in front of the bier has been identified with Beneš (Benesch)
Krabice of Veitmile (Weitmuehl), chronicler and canon of St. Vitus'
Cathedral in Prague in the time of Charles IV.

Former Collection: Counts Kolowrat, Košátky Castle, Bohemia.
References: A. Matejček, *Czech Gothic Painting* (Prague, 1950), pp. 48 ff.,
pls. 38–41; Hanns Swarzenski, "A Masterpiece of Bohemian Art," MFA
Bulletin 50, no. 282 (1952), pp. 63–74.

6

Man of Sorrows
Alsatian, 15th century
Oil on panel, 27^{1}/$_{4}$ × 15^{1}/$_{4}$ in.
Gift in Memory of W. G. Russell Allen by his Friends 56.262

The subject is one of the devotional images (*Andachtsbilder*) derived
from the Passion and intended for private devotional contemplation.
The style of this panel suggests a painter of the Alsatian School
active in Colmar or Strasbourg around 1460–70.

Reference: Hanns Swarzenski, "A Painting of the Man of Sorrows,"
MFA *Bulletin* 54, no. 298 (Winter 1956), pp. 82–87.

5

6

7

ROGIER VAN DER WEYDEN, Flemish, ca. 1399–1464
St. Luke Painting the Virgin
Oil on panel, 54¹/₄ × 43³/₄ in.
Gift of Mr. and Mrs. Henry Lee Higginson 93.153

This painting representing the apocryphal subject of St. Luke making a portrait of the Virgin was the first important early Flemish work to enter an American public collection. It was executed shortly after Rogier's arrival in Brussels in 1435 and probably was the altarpiece which the artist is supposed to have painted for the Painters' Guild. The figure of St. Luke may represent an idealized self-portrait of the artist in the role of head of his guild.

Former Collections: Don Sebastian-Gabriel Bórbon y Braganza, Spain; Queen Isabella II of Spain; Don Pedro, Duke of Dúrcal, Spain; Henry Lee Higginson, Boston.
References: M. Friedländer, *Die altniederländische Malerei*, II (Berlin, 1924), no. 106 c, p. 127; Philip Hendy, "S. Luke Drawing the Virgin, by Roger van der Weyden," MFA *Bulletin* 31, no. 187 (October 1933), pp. 74–75; E. Panofsky, *Early Netherlandish Painting: Its Origin and Character* (Cambridge, Mass., 1953), pp. 252–54, fig. 313; Detroit Institute of Arts, *Flanders in the Fifteenth Century; Art and Civilization,* (Antwerp, 1960), no. 7, pp. 76–80; Colin Eisler, *New England Museums* (vol. 4 of *Les Primitifs Flamands*, Brussels, 1961), pp. 71–93.

7

8

The Martyrdom of St. Hippolytus
Flemish, last quarter of the 15th century
Oil on panel, 39¹/₂ × 115 in. overall
Purchased 63.660

Commissioned by Hippolytus de Berthoz, financial advisor to Philip
the Good, Duke of Burgundy, this triptych relates in its rare subject
matter to an earlier panel painting of the martyrdom of St. Hippolytus by Dieric Bouts, ordered by the same donor. This work, stylis-
tically very different, was made into a triptych by the addition of
side panels representing de Berthoz and his wife by Hugo van der
Goes. In the Boston triptych which came to light in 1962, the inter-
pretation of the martyrdom appears to be based on a poem commissioned by de Berthoz from Jean Molinet, chronicler of the Burgun-
dian court. Four saints are painted in *grisaille* on the outside wings:
on the right St. Bavo of Ghent and St. Elizabeth of Hungary; on the
left, St. Catherine of Alexandria and probably St. Thomas à Becket.

The family arms of de Berthoz appear on each wing: undifferenced on the left, and impaled on the right with those of Elizabeth van Keverwyck, first wife of Hippolytus de Berthoz.

Former Collections: Émile Gavet, Paris; Lucien Félix Claude-Lafontaine, Paris.

8 right wing

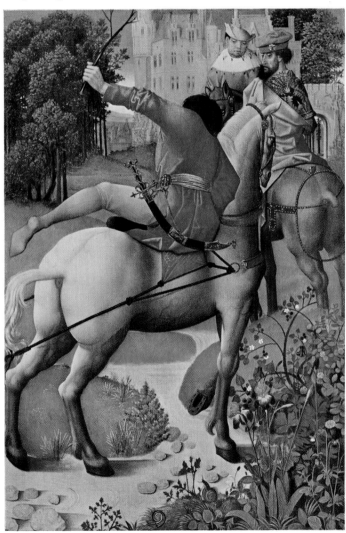

9

9

Virgin and Child with a Donor
Valencian, 15th century
Tempera on panel, 57¹/₄ × 30¹/₂ in.
Maria Antoinette Evans Fund 29.1129

This panel was apparently the central part of a retable painted about 1400. It belongs to the Valencian group which represents the collaboration of Pedro Nicolau and Marzal de Sas.

Former Collection: From cathedral of Jàtiva, Valencia, Spain.
Reference: Chandler R. Post, *History of Spanish Painting* (Cambridge, 1933), vol. 4, pt. 2, pp. 541, 580–83, 590.

10

GIOVANNI DI PAOLO, Sienese, ca. 1403–1483
The Virgin of Humility
Tempera on panel, 22 × 17 in.
Maria Antoinette Evans Fund 30.772

An early work under the influence of Sassetta, this panel probably dates from about 1440.

Former Collection: Dr. Albert Figdor, Vienna.
References: Philip Hendy, "Giovanni di Paolo," MFA *Bulletin* 28, no. 170 (December 1930), pp. 103–04; John Pope-Hennessy, *Giovanni di Paolo* (London, 1937), pp. 27–28.

11

BRAMANTINO (BARTOLOMMEO SUARDI), Milanese, ca. 1465–1530
Virgin and Child
Tempera on panel, 18⅛ × 14 in.
Purchased 13.2859

The Milanese painter of this panel was an intimate friend of the great painter-architect Bramante and his style so closely emulated that of his friend that he was given the name of Bramantino, "the little Bramante." The *Virgin and Child* may date as early as about 1495 and is a fundamental work in the formative period of the artist.

Former Collection: P. M. Turner, London.
Reference: Jean Guiffrey, "Madonna and Child, Bramantino," MFA *Bulletin* 11, no. 67 (December 1913), pp. 67–68.

10

II

12

Presentation of the Virgin in the Temple
Master of the Barberini Panels, Italian, second half of the 15th
century
Tempera on panel, 58 × 38¹/₂ in.
Charles Potter Kling Fund 37.108

Before entering the Barberini Collection in Rome, this painting was
probably part of the paneling of the ducal palace in Urbino during
the reign of Federigo da Montefeltro. Together with its pendant,
the *Birth of the Virgin* (now in The Metropolitan Museum), it has
been the subject of numerous attributions: Fra Carnevale, Giovanni
Angelo di Antonio, and the painter-architects Bramante and Alberti.

Former Collections: Barberini Collection, Rome; Prince Corsini,
Florence.
References: Charles C. Cunningham, "A Great Renaissance Panel,"
MFA *Bulletin* 35, no. 210 (August 1937), pp. 45–50; Richard Offner,
"The Barberini Panels and their Painter," *Mediaeval Studies in Memory
of A. Kingsley Porter* (Cambridge, 1939), pp. 205–53; Georg Swarzenski,
"The Master of the Barberini Panels: Bramante," MFA *Bulletin* 38,
no. 230 (December 1940), pp. 90–97; Alessandro Parronchi, "Leon Bat-
tista Alberti as a Painter," *Burlington Magazine* 104 (July 1962),
pp. 280–86.

12

13

Marriage Salver (Desco da parto)
Ferrarese, 15th century
Tempera on panel, dodecagonal, 24 × 24 in.
Gift of Mrs. Walter Scott Fitz 17.198

The obverse of this panel shows "Solomon and the Queen of Sheba," the reverse "A Cupid with Emblems of Prosperity." The work was probably painted by an artist, possibly a miniaturist, working in Ferrara under the influence of Francesco del Cossa and Ercole Roberti. The main side recalls the style of Taddeo Crivelli; the reverse is more reminiscent of Cossa's influence.

Former Collections: E. Secrétan, Paris; Count Chabrières-Arlès, Paris; Mrs. Walter Scott Fitz, Boston.
Reference: Bernard Berenson, *Essays in the Study of Sienese Painting* (New York, 1918), p. 57.

14

LORENZO LOTTO, Venetian, ca. 1480–1556
Madonna and Child with St. Jerome and St. Anthony of Padua
Oil on canvas, 37 × 30¹/₂ in.
Charles Potter Kling Fund 60.154

The composition is identical with an inferior and less well-preserved version in the National Gallery, London, signed and dated 1521.

Former Collection: Professor R. M. Dawkins, Oxford, England.
Reference: Cecil Gould, *The Sixteenth Century Venetian Schools* (National Gallery Catalogues, London, 1959), p. 53.

15

15

TITIAN (TIZIANO VECELLIO), Venetian, ca. 1487/90–1576
St. Catherine of Alexandria
Signed at lower left on stone: . . *TIANUS · F ·*
Oil on canvas, 46³/₈ × 39¹/₄ in.
Purchase Fund and Otis Norcross Fund 48.499

Former Collections: Lord Radstock, England; Leopold Koppel, Berlin.
References: Erica Tietze-Conrat, "Titian's St. Catherine," *Gazette des Beaux-Arts,* 6th series, 43 (April 1954), pp. 257–61; Joy Kenseth, "Titian's St. Catherine of Alexandria," MFA *Bulletin* 67, no. 350 (1969), pp. 175–88.

16

16

TINTORETTO (JACOPO ROBUSTI), Venetian, 1518–1594
Alessandro Farnese
Oil on canvas, 24⅝ × 21 in.
Gift of Mrs. Walter Scott Fitz and Robert Treat Paine, 2nd 27.862

The portrait represents a young man of about fifteen to eighteen
years. If it is indeed Prince Alessandro Farnese, regent of the Nether-
lands under Philip II of Spain, it must have been painted around
1560–65; should it, however, be Prince Luigi (Aloysius) Gonzaga,
later canonized as a Jesuit saint, then it must date from 1580–85.

Former Collection: Sir Richard Waldie-Griffith, Hendersyde Park, Kelso,
Scotland.
References: Philip Hendy, "Paintings by Tintoretto in Boston," *Burlington
Magazine* 42 (March 1933), pp. 129 ff.; Hans Tietze, *Tintoretto, The
Paintings and Drawings* (New York, 1948), p. 347.

17

IL ROSSO FIORENTINO, Florentine, 1494–1540
The Dead Christ with Angels
Signed on sarcophagus at lower right: *Rubeus / Flo / Faciebat*
Oil on panel, 52½ × 40¾ in.
Charles Potter Kling Fund 58.527

Dating from Rosso's Roman period between 1524–27, this painting
recorded by Vasari is the only complete work in America by the
great Florentine Mannerist.

Former Collections: Probably the picture mentioned by Vasari as painted
by Rosso for his friend the bishop of San Sepolcro, Leonardo Tornabuoni;
Giovanni della Casa; Bórbon family, Spain.
References: Vasari, *Vite*, vol. V, p. 162 (edition of 1568). John Shearman,
"The 'Dead Christ' by Rosso Fiorentino," MFA *Bulletin* 64, no. 338 (1966),
pp. 148–72.

17

18

LUCAS VAN LEYDEN, Dutch, 1494–1533
Moses Striking the Rock in the Wilderness
Signed and dated on rock at left of center: *L 1527*
Tempera on canvas, 70³/₄ × 92 in.
William K. Richardson Fund 54.1432

Paintings by this great engraver of the Northern Renaissance are not
numerous. This is his only extant painting on canvas, and one of the
three dated works of his mature years, the others being in Leyden
(1526) and the Hermitage, Leningrad (1531).

Former Collections: Galleria Borghese, Rome; Princess di Piombino,
Rome; Germanisches Nationalmuseum, Nuremberg.
References: M. Friedländer, *Die altniederländische Malerei* (Leiden, 1932),
no. 116, p. 99; — *Lucas van Leyden* (Berlin, 1963), p. 66.

19

PAOLO VERONESE, Venetian, 1528–1588
Diana and Actaeon
Venus and Jupiter
Olympus (not illus.)
Atalanta and Meleager (not illus.)
Oil on canvas, 10 × 43¹/₂ in.
Gifts and Bequests of Mrs. Edward Jackson Holmes 59.260, 60.125,
64.2078, 64.2079

These four panels of mythological subjects must have formed part
of the decoration of a room. They are in Veronese's early style of
painting on a small scale, and probably date from around 1560.

Former Collections: Holford Collection, Dorchester House, London.
References: The Holford Collection (Oxford, 1927), I, p. 41, no. 82, repr.
(*Diana and Actaeon*), p. 42, no. 83, repr. (*Atalanta and Meleager*).

20

ANTONIO CANALE (CANALETTO), Venetian, 1697–1768
Bacino di San Marco, Venice
Oil on canvas, 49¹/₈ × 60¹/₄ in.
Abbot Lawrence Fund, Seth K. Sweetser Fund, and Charles Edward
French Fund 39.290

Painted probably in the 1730's and acquired shortly thereafter by
either the fourth or the fifth Earl of Carlisle, the painting is in all
probability but one collection removed from Canaletto's easel.

Former Collection: Earls of Carlisle, Castle Howard, Yorkshire.
References: W. G. Constable, "The Bacino di San Marco, by Antonio
Canale," MFA *Bulletin* 37, no. 219 (June 1939), pp. 47–50; —, *Canaletto*
(Oxford, 1962), vol. 2, no. 131.

21

FRANCESCO GUARDI, Venetian, 1712–1793
Reception of a Dignitary
Oil on canvas, 38³/₄ × 54³/₈ in.
Picture Fund 11.1451

Former Collections: Captain Harvey, London; Baron Lazzaroni, Paris.
References: G. Fiocco, *Francesco Guardi* (Florence, 1923), p. 73, no. 78,
pl. LXVI; P. Zampetti, *Mostra dei Guardi* (Venice, 1965), p. 291, no. 151,
repr.

22

EL GRECO (DOMENIKOS THEOTOKOPOULOS), Spanish,
1541–1614
Fray Felix Hortensio Paravicino
Signed in Greek at center of right edge: *domēnikos theotokopoulos
epoiei*
Oil on canvas, 44^{1}/$_{2}$ × 33^{7}/$_{8}$ in.
Isaac Sweetser Fund 04.234

Fray Felix, a Trinitarian canon, was professor of rhetoric at the
University of Salamanca at the age of twenty-one and preacher to
King Philip III of Spain. His intimate friend El Greco painted this
likeness of him at the age of twenty-nine, in 1609. In response Paravicino composed four sonnets addressed to the painter, "the rival
of Prometheus." John Singer Sargent recommended the painting
for purchase.

Former Collections: Duke of Arcos, Madrid; Don Fray Javier de
Muguiro, Madrid.
References: M. B. Cossio, *El Greco* (Madrid, 1908), pp. 439 ff., no. 278;
A. Mayer, *El Greco* (Munich, 1926), pp. 33–34, no. 335 a; Harold Wethey,
El Greco and His School (Princeton, 1962), vol. 2, p. 95.

22

23

23

DIEGO VELÁZQUEZ, Spanish, 1599–1660
Don Baltasar Carlos and His Dwarf
Oil on canvas, 53^{1}/$_{2}$ × 41 in.
Henry Lillie Pierce Fund 01.104

Don Baltasar Carlos (1629–1646), the elder son of Philip IV of Spain by his first wife, Elizabeth of France, was first portrayed in this work by Velázquez. Painted immediately upon the artist's return from his first trip to Italy in 1631, it shows the young prince at one year, four months of age, as is borne out by the inscription on the curtain (*Aetatis An... Mens 4*).

Former Collection: Earls of Carlisle, Castle Howard, Yorkshire.
References: F. Pacheco, *Arte de la Pintura* (Seville, 1649), vol. 1, p. 105; Elizabeth du Gue Trapier, *Velázquez* (New York, 1948), pp. 171–76; J. Lopez-Rey, *Velázquez: A Catalogue Raisonné* (London, 1963), no. 302.

24

PETER PAUL RUBENS, Flemish, 1577–1640
The Head of Cyrus Brought to Queen Tomyris
Oil on canvas, 80$\frac{1}{2}$ × 141 in.
Robert J. Edwards Fund 41.40

The subject was taken from Herodotus' account of the war between
the Persians and the Massegetae, "one of the stubbornest of all
fights that were ever fought by men that were not Greek." For his
painting Rubens chose the climactic moment when Tomyris, queen
of the Massegetae, takes revenge for the death of her son by causing
the head of Cyrus, king of the Persians, to be bathed in blood. The
subject probably illustrates the vice of insatiability, while the companion painting, *Scipio* (no longer extant), represented the corres-
ponding virtue of abstinence. The painting can be dated 1620–1622
on the basis of the ages of the painter's sons, Albert and Nicholas,
who appear as the queen's trainbearers. The collaboration of Jacob
Jordaens, Van Dyck, and Frans Snyders, all members of Rubens'
studio, is evident in this work.

Former Collections: Queen Christina of Sweden, Stockholm and Rome;
Cardinal Deccio Azzolini, Rome; Odescalchi family, Rome; Dukes of
Orléans, Paris; Earl of Darnley, Cobham Hall, Kent; sixth Earl of Hare-
wood, Harewood House, Yorkshire.
References: Charles C. Cunningham, "A Great Rubens Comes to the
Museum," MFA *Bulletin* 39, no. 233 (June 1941), pp. 35–40; J.-A. Goris
and J. Held, *Rubens in America* (New York, 1947), p. 39, no. 83; W. G.
Constable, "Rubens in the Museum of Fine Arts, Boston," *Miscellanea
Leo van Puyvelde* (Brussels, 1949), pp. 131–32.

24

25

PETER PAUL RUBENS, Flemish, 1577–1640
Portrait of Mulay Ahmad
Oil on panel, 39^1/$_2$ × 28 in.
Maria Theresa Burnham Hopkins Fund 40.2

This Rubens portrait painted about 1610 is a free copy of a lost
painting by Jan Cornelisz Vermeyen (1500–1559). The sitter is
Mulay Ahmad, son of Mulay Hasan, Berber king of Tunis. Vermeyen's portrait of the African prince was painted in 1535 when the
artist accompanied Emperor Charles V on his campaign in Tunis.
This portrait was probably in Rubens' own collection erroneously
attributed to Antonio Moro (Anthonis Mor).

Former Collections: Rubens' estate; Duke of Wellington (Wellesley Collection); Marquis du Blaisel; E. Secrétan, Paris; John Wanamaker, Philadelphia.
References: Julius S. Held, "Rubens' 'King of Tunis' and Vermeyen's Portrait of Mulay Ahmad," *Art Quarterly* 3 (1940), pp. 173–81.

25

26 27

REMBRANDT VAN RIJN, Dutch, 1606–1669
The Rev. Johannes Elison
Mrs. Johannes Elison (Maria Bockenolle)
Each signed and dated lower right: *Rembrandt· f: ·1634·*
Oil on canvas, $68^1/8$ and $68^3/4 \times 48^7/8$ in.
William K. Richardson Fund 56.510 and 56.511

Elison was the pastor of the Dutch Reformed Church in Norwich, England. The two portraits were commissioned by the eldest son of the sitters, who was a prosperous businessman in Amsterdam. On a visit to their son in Amsterdam the parents sat for the twenty-eight-year-old Rembrandt.

Former Collections: Johannes Elison the younger, Amsterdam; Samuel Colby, his descendant, Yarmouth; Eugène Schneider, Paris.
References: Jakob Rosenberg, "Rembrandt's Portraits of Johannes Elison and His Wife," MFA *Bulletin* 45, no. 299 (Spring 1957), pp. 3–9.

28

31

LUIS EGIDIO MELÉNDEZ (or MENÉNDEZ), Spanish,
1716–1780
Still Life with Bread, Bacon, and Vegetables
Oil on canvas, 25 × 33½ in.
Margaret Curry Wyman Fund 39.40

His skill as a painter of still lifes won Meléndez the epithet of the
"Spanish Chardin." Like the majority of his still lifes, this one probably dates from about 1772.

Reference: Martin Soria, *Art and Architecture in Spain and Portugal and
their American Dominions, 1500 to 1800* (Pelican History of Art Series,
London and Baltimore, 1959), p. 299, pl. 163 B.

32

FRANCISCO ZURBARAN, Spanish, 1598–1664
St. Peter Thomas
St. Cyril
Oil on canvas, 36½ × 12¾ in.; 36½ × 13 in.
Gifts of Mrs. Zoe Oliver Sherman 23.554 and 22.642

Both paintings were probably part of an altarpiece painted around
1630–32 for the Carmelite church of San Alberto in Seville. The
saints represented were both Carmelites: St. Peter Thomas (d. 1366)
was archbishop of Crete and Latin patriarch of Constantinople;
St. Cyril (d. 1225) was the third general of the Carmelite Order.

Former Collections: Alcazar, Seville; Duke of Sutherland, Stafford House,
London; Zoe Oliver Sherman, Boston.
Reference: Martin S. Soria, *The Paintings of Zurbaran* (London, 1953),
p. 142, nos. 42, 43.

33

NICOLAS POUSSIN, French, 1594–1665
Mars and Venus
Oil on canvas, 61 × 84 in.
Augustus Hemenway and Arthur Wheelwright Funds 40.89

This work of Poussin's early Roman years probably dates from just before 1630. The classical subject was taken from either *De rerum natura* of Lucretius or the *Thebaid* of Statius. The Titianesque landscape marks the brief period of Venetian influence in the artist's career.

Former Collections: Probably painted for Cassiano dal Pozzo; Henry Furness, England; first Earl of Harcourt, Nuneham Park, Oxford.
References: Charles C. Cunningham, "Poussin's Mars and Venus," MFA *Bulletin* 38, no. 228 (August 1940), pp. 55–58; Walter Friedländer, *Nicolas Poussin, A New Approach* (New York, 1964), p. 118; Anthony Blunt, *The Paintings of Nicolas Poussin* (London, 1966), no. 183.

34

34

CLAUDE LORRAIN, French, 1600–1682
Parnassus
Signed and dated bottom center: *Claudio IV fecit 168[0]*
Oil on canvas, 38½ × 53 in.
Picture Fund 12.1050

Between 1663 and 1682 Claude recorded in his *Liber veritatis* (the personal catalogue of his works) eight paintings, including *Parnassus*, made for Prince Lorenzo Onofrio Colonna, grand constable of the kingdom of Naples, and Claude's most important patron in Rome.

Former Collections: Colonna Gallery, Rome; Sloane, Rome; Walsh Porter, London; Rev. Holwell Carr, London; Aynard (Eynard), Paris; Wynn Ellis, London; William Graham; Sir William Farrar.
References: Liber veritatis, no. 193; Jean Guiffrey, "The Parnassus of Claude Gellée," MFA *Bulletin* 11, no. 61 (February 1913), p. 9; Marcel Röthlisberger, *Claude Lorrain: The Paintings* (New Haven, 1961), vol. 1, pp. 451–52 and vol. 2, fig. 314.

35

GEORGE ROMNEY, British, 1734–1802
Anne, Lady de la Pole
Oil on canvas, 95½ × 59 in.
Given in Memory of Governor Alvan T. Fuller by the Fuller Foundation 61.392

Anne was the only daughter of John Templar, Esq., of Stover House, Devonshire. She married Sir John William de la Pole, sixth Baronet, in January, 1781. Sittings of Sir John, whose portrait is in the Wadsworth Athenaeum, Hartford, and of Lady de la Pole are recorded in Romney's diary from January to May 1786.

Former Collections: Sir Frederick Arundel de la Pole, Shute House, Axminster, Devonshire; Gov. Alvan T. Fuller, Boston.
Reference: Thomas Humphrey Ward and W. Roberts, *Romney, A Biographical and Critical Essay* (London, 1904), vol. 2, p. 124 (erroneously listed as half-lengths).

35

36

THOMAS GAINSBOROUGH, British, 1727–1788
Captain Thomas Mathews
Oil on canvas, 29³/₄ × 24¹/₂ in.
Juliana Cheney Edwards Collection 25.134

Gainsborough set up his studio in the fashionable resort of Bath between 1760 and 1774, and it was during this period that he painted the well-known dilettante, Captain Mathews. Thomas Mathews was Richard Brinsley Sheridan's antagonist in the courtship of the "Maid of Bath," Miss Elizabeth Linley. When Sheridan eloped with Miss Linley, Mathews attacked him in an advertisement in the Bath Chronicle of April 9, 1772. Within a few days of the appearance of this advertisement Mathews left Bath, and probably it is owing to this unexpected departure that Gainsborough was unable to put the finishing touches to the portrait. The companion portrait of Mrs. Mathews is also in the Museum's collection.

Former Collections: Jones family, descendants of the sitter's wife, Fonmon Castle, Cowbridge, S. Wales; Robert J. Edwards, Boston.
Reference: Ellis K. Waterhouse, *Gainsborough* (London, 1958), no. 473.

37

JEAN-BAPTISTE SIMÉON CHARDIN, French, 1699–1779
The Teapot
Signed and dated lower left: *Chardin / 1764*
Oil on canvas, 12⁵/₈ × 15⁷/₈ in.
Gift of Martin Brimmer 83.177

In 1883 this still life became the first work of Chardin to enter an American public collection.

Former Collections: Baron de Beurnonville; Martin Brimmer, Boston.
Reference: Georges Wildenstein, *Chardin* (Zurich, 1963), p. 209, no. 335.

36

37

38

JEAN-HONORÉ FRAGONARD, French, 1732–1806
La Bonne Mère (The Good Mother)
Oil on canvas, 25¹/₄ × 20³/₄ in.
Bequest of Robert Treat Paine, 2nd 44.777

The mother is traditionally said to be Marie-Anne Gérard, whom Fragonard married in 1769. These "scenes of family life" date between 1777 and 1779.

Former Collections: F. Spitzer, Paris; Mme. Pellegrin; R. S. Bertron, New York; R. T. Paine, 2nd, Boston.
Reference: Georges Wildenstein, *The Paintings of Fragonard* (London, 1960), p. 299, no. 451.

39

ANTOINE WATTEAU, French, 1684–1721
La Perspective (The Vista)
Oil on canvas, 18¹/₂ × 22 in.
Maria Antoinette Evans Fund 23.573

The scene is set in the gardens of the Château de Luxembourg at Montmorency, which was owned by Pierre Crozat, Watteau's friend and patron. The work probably dates between 1716 and 1718 when the artist was a guest at Montmorency.

Former Collections: M. Guénon, Paris; Sir Richard Wallace, London.
References: Edmond and Jules de Goncourt, *French XVIIIth Century Painters,* trans. Robin Ironside (London, 1948), p. 39; Charles H. Hawes, "'La Perspective' by Antoine Watteau," MFA *Bulletin* 22, no. 129 (February 1924), pp. 1–2.

40

FRANÇOIS BOUCHER, French, 1703–1770
The Halt at the Spring
Signed and dated at middle right on pedestal: *Boucher 1765*
Oil on canvas, 82½ × 108¼ in.
Gift of the Heirs of Peter Parker 71.2

45

46

JEAN-BAPTISTE CAMILLE COROT, French, 1796–1875
Island of San Bartolommeo, Rome
Signed lower right: *Corot*
Oil on canvas, 10¹/₂ × 17 in.
Harriet Otis Cruft Fund 23.118

This early work of about 1827, painted on his first trip to Rome, reveals Corot as a precursor of Cubism.

Former Collection: Pierre Hentsch, Paris.
Reference: Charles C. Cunningham, "Some Corot Paintings in the Museum's Collection," MFA *Bulletin* 34, no. 206 (December 1936), pp. 99–100.

47

HENRI FANTIN-LATOUR, French, 1836–1904
Flowers and Fruit
Signed and dated lower right: *Fantin 1865*
Oil on canvas 23¹/₂ × 28³/₄ in.
Bequest of John T. Spaulding 48.540

Former Collections: From the artist's collection; Ch. de Hèle, Brussels;
Julien Tempelaere, Paris; A. Reid, Glasgow; Cargill Collection, Scotland;
John T. Spaulding, Boston.

48

48

JOSEPH MALLORD WILLIAM TURNER, British, 1775–1851
The Slave Ship
Oil on canvas, 35 ³/₄ × 48 in.
Henry Lillie Pierce Fund 99.22

Turner's sources for the subject were a passage in Thomson's
"Seasons" and a published account of an actual incident which
occurred in 1783. The historical event concerned slave victims of an
epidemic being thrown overboard, rather than allowed to die on
ship, because insurance could be claimed only on those actually
"lost at sea." After being exhibited at the Royal Academy in 1840,
the painting became the center of a controversy. It disturbed the
young Thackeray, George Inness, and Mark Twain, the last de-
scribing it as "a tortoise-shell cat having a fit in a platter of toma-
toes." John Ruskin, however, thought it "the noblest sea that Turner
ever painted.... I believe, if I were reduced to rest Turner's immor-
tality upon any single work, I should choose this."

Former Collections: Purchased from Turner by John Ruskin, Sr., and
given to his son; John Taylor Johnston, New York; Miss Alice Hooper,
Boston; W. H. S. Lothrop, Boston.
References: Arts Council of Great Britain, *The Romantic Movement*
(London, 1959), no. 357; J. Rothenstein and M. Butlin, *Turner* (New York,
1964), pp. 58–60.

49

JEAN FRANÇOIS MILLET, French, 1814–1875
Young Shepherdess
Oil on canvas, 64 × 44¹/₄ in.
Gift of Samuel Dennis Warren 77.249

The largest of sixty-eight paintings by Millet in the Museum's
collections is this late work of about 1869–71. The sitter is his
daughter, Marguerite.

Former Collection: Samuel D. Warren, Boston.
Reference: Robert L. Herbert, *Barbizon Revisited* (Boston, 1962), p. 152,
no. 77.

49

50

HONORÉ DAUMIER, French, 1808–1879
L'Homme à la corde (The Man on the Rope)
Oil on canvas, $44^{1}/_{2} \times 28^{1}/_{2}$ in.
Arthur Gordon Tompkins Residuary Fund 43.31

Also known under the title, *Le Badigeonneur* (The Whitewasher or The House Painter) and *L'Évasion* (Escape), the subject of the painting is uncertain. One of three versions, it is unfinished and probably dates between 1858 and 1860.

Former Collections: M. Hazard, Orrouy, France; Joseph Kerrigan, New York.
Reference: K. E. Maison, *Honoré Daumier, Catalogue raisonné* (New York, 1968), vol. 1, p. 117, no. 123.

51

EDGAR DEGAS, French, 1834–1917
Duke and Duchess of Morbilli
Oil on canvas, $45^{3}/_{4} \times 35^{1}/_{4}$ in.
Gift of Robert Treat Paine, 2nd 31.33

Duke Edmondo Morbilli, a banker, was born in 1836 in Naples and died there in 1894. In 1863 a special dispensation from the pope allowed him to marry his first cousin, the artist's sister Thérèse, who was born in 1840 in Naples and died there in 1897. The portrait shown here was painted in 1867 while the artist was in Italy. A drawing of Thérèse and a preliminary study for the head of Edmondo are also in the Museum.

Former Collections: René de Gas, Paris; Robert Treat Paine, 2nd, Boston.
References: Philip Hendy, "Degas and the de Gas," MFA *Bulletin 30* (June 1932), p. 44–45; P. A. Lemoisne, *Degas et son œuvre* (Paris, 1946), vol. 2, no. 164, repr.; Jean S. Boggs, *Portraits by Degas* (Berkeley, 1962), pp. 17–18; Daniel Catton Rich, *Degas* (New York, 1966), p. 42.

50

51

52

EDGAR DEGAS, French, 1834–1917
Carriage at the Races
Signed lower left: *Degas*
Oil on canvas, 13³/4 × 21³/8 in.
Arthur Gordon Tompkins Residuary Fund 26.790

In this painting of about 1872 Degas represented his friend Paul
Valpinçon and his family. The composition is strongly influenced by
Japanese prints. It was included in the first Impressionist exhibition
in 1874.

Former Collections: Jean-Baptiste Faure, Paris; Durand-Ruel, Paris.
References: A. C. Jenks, "Carriages at the Races," MFA *Bulletin* 25,
no. 147 (February 1927), pp. 2–3; P. A. Lemoisne, *Degas et son œuvre*
(Paris, 1946), vol. 1, p. 85, repr. opp. p. 70, vol. 2, p. 281; Jean S. Boggs,
Portraits by Degas (Berkeley, 1962), pp. 37, 46; Aaron Scharf, "Painting,
Photography, and the Image of Movement," *Burlington Magazine* 104
(May 1962), p. 191; Daniel Catton Rich, *Degas* (New York, 1966), p. 50.

53

ÉDOUARD MANET, French, 1832–1883
The Street Singer
Signed at lower left: *Ed. Manet*
Oil on canvas, 69 × 42³/₄ in.
Bequest of Sarah Choate Sears in Memory of her Husband, Joshua
Montgomery Sears 66.304

This work of about 1862 is one of the earliest paintings posed for by
Victorine-Louise Meurend, Manet's frequent and favorite model
between 1862 and 1875. The painting was a favorite of Manet's
friend, Émile Zola.

Former Collections: Ernest Hoschedé, Paris; Jean-Baptiste Faure, Paris;
Mrs. J. Montgomery Sears, Boston.
References: Étienne Moreau-Nélaton, *Manet raconté par lui-même*
(Paris, 1924), no. 37; Jamot-Wildenstein, *Manet* (Paris, 1932), no. 45,
fig. 37.

54

ÉDOUARD MANET, French, 1832–1883
Victorine Meurend
Signed at upper right: *Manet*
Oil on canvas, 17 × 17 in.
Gift of Richard C. Paine in Memory of his Father, Robert Treat
Paine, 2nd 46.846

Manet met the sitter by chance in a crowd at the Palais de Justice,
Paris. This portrait dates from around 1862. She was to become the
model for such major works as *Déjeuner sur l'herbe* (1863) and
Olympia (1865).

Former Collections: Sir William Burrell, Glasgow; Alphonse Kann, Paris;
Robert Treat Paine, 2nd, Boston.
References: E. Moreau-Nélaton, *Manet raconté par lui-même* (Paris,
1924), no. 77; Jamot-Wildenstein, *Manet* (Paris, 1932), no. 50, fig. 33.

53

54

55

55

CLAUDE MONET, French, 1840–1926
La Japonaise
Signed and dated lower left: *Claude Monet 1876*
1951 Purchase Fund 56.147

Monet began collecting Japanese prints at the age of seventeen.
Beginning with this painting of 1876, the oriental influence becomes
increasingly evident in his work. Monet wrote about this picture:
"It is not a painting of a Japanese, but rather of a French girl in
Japanese costume—it was my first wife who posed for me."

Former Collections: Ernest Hoschedé, Paris; Count Jean de Rasti, Paris;
Philip Lehman, New York.
References: G. Geffroy, *Claude Monet* (Paris, 1922), pp. 59–73; William
Seitz, *Claude Monet* (New York, 1960), pp. 104–5.

56

CLAUDE MONET, French, 1840–1926
Village Street, Normandy
Signed lower left: *Claude Monet*
Oil on canvas, 22 × 24 in.
Bequest of John T. Spaulding 48.580

Painted about 1865–66, the view is probably of the Rue de la Ba-
volle, Honfleur.

Former Collections: Oscar Schmitz, Dresden; John T. Spaulding, Boston.
Reference: John Rewald, *History of Impressionism* (New York, 1961),
p. 128.

56

57

CLAUDE MONET, French, 1840–1926
The Old Fort at Antibes
Signed and dated lower left: *Claude Monet 88*
Oil on canvas, 26 × 32 in.
Gift of Samuel Dacre Bush 27.1324

This impressionistic view of Antibes was painted in the spring of
1888. Mallarmé said of Monet's Antibes period: "This is your finest
hour."

Former Collection: Samuel Dacre Bush, Boston.
Reference: William Seitz, *Claude Monet* (New York, 1960), pp. 134–35.

58

ALFRED SISLEY, French, 1839–1899
Early Snow at Louveciennes
Signed lower right: *A. Sisley*
Oil on canvas, 21¼ × 28¾ in.
Bequest of John T. Spaulding 48.600

During the siege of Paris, Sisley took refuge in Voisins-Louve-
ciennes, remaining there until 1874. This work probably dates from
the winter of 1870.

Former Collections: Picq-Veron, Ermont-Eaubonne; National-Galerie,
Berlin; John T. Spaulding, Boston.
Reference: F. Daulte, *Alfred Sisley, Catalogue Raisonné* (Lausanne, 1959),
no. 18, repr.

59

CAMILLE PISSARRO, French, 1830–1903
Market Place, Gisors
Signed and dated at lower right: *C. Pissarro 1885*
Gouache and pastel on mounted paper, $32^{1}/_{4} \times 32^{1}/_{4}$ in.
Bequest of John T. Spaulding 48.588

This opaque watercolor of the poultry market in Gisors was done in 1885.

Former Collections: Claude Monet, Giverny; Michel Monet, Giverny; John T. Spaulding, Boston.
Reference: L. Pissarro, *Camille Pissarro* (Paris, 1939), no. 1400, p. 275, pl. 273.

60

60

PIERRE AUGUSTE RENOIR, French, 1841–1919
Le Bal à Bougival
Signed and dated lower right: *Renoir, '83*
Oil on canvas, 70⁵/₈ × 37³/₄ in.
Anna Mitchell Richards Fund and Contributions 37.375

The painting is one of three dance pictures executed by Renoir in 1883. Suzanne Valadon, a painter, model, and mother of Maurice Utrillo, posed with Renoir's brother.

Former Collections: François Depeaux, Mesnil-Esnard; Barret-Décap, Biarritz; Anthony H. Manley, Paris.
References: J. Meier-Graefe, *Renoir* (Leipzig, 1929), p. 172, fig. 157; James S. Plaut, "A Great Renoir," MFA *Bulletin* 35, no. 209 (June 1937), pp. 29–33; M. Drucker, *Renoir* (Paris, 1944), p. 64, pl. 75.

61

PIERRE AUGUSTE RENOIR, French, 1841–1919
Les Enfants à Guernesey (Children on the Seashore)
Signed lower right: *Renoir*
Oil on canvas, 36 × 26¹/₄ in.
John T. Spaulding Bequest 48.594

This painting should probably be dated 1883 or later, as there is no evidence that Renoir went to Guernsey before that year.

Former Collections: Galerie Barbazanges, Paris (bought from the descendants of Renoir after his death, from the studio); John T. Spaulding, Boston.
Reference: J. Meier-Graefe, *Renoir* (Leipzig, 1929), p. 180, repr. no. 151.

61

62

PAUL CÉZANNE, French, 1839–1906
Madame Cézanne in a Red Armchair
Oil on canvas, 28¹/₂ × 22 in.
Bequest of Robert Treat Paine, 2nd 44.776

Marie-Hortense Fiquet was Cézanne's mistress from about 1871
and bore him a son, Paul, in January, 1872. He married her in April,
1886. This portrait, painted about 1877, is one of twenty-seven oils
Cézanne painted of her over a period of about thirty years.

Former Collections: Egisto Fabbri, Florence; Samuel Courtauld, London;
Robert Treat Paine, 2nd, Boston.
References: L. Venturi, *Cézanne – son art – son œuvre* (Paris, 1936), vol. 1,
no. 292, p. 128, vol. 2, pl. 79; Bernard Dorival, *Cézanne* (New York, 1948),
no. 45, p. 143 (quotes R. M. Rilke's description from *Letters on Cézanne*);
Anne H. van Buren, "Madame Cézanne's Fashions and the Dates of Her
Portraits," *Art Quarterly* 29, no. 2 (1966), pp. 111–27.

63

PAUL CÉZANNE, French, 1839–1906
L'Étang (The Pond)
Oil on canvas, 18¹/₂ × 22¹/₂ in.
Arthur Gordon Tompkins Residuary Fund 48.244

The spatial organization of this painting of about 1873–75 is almost
identical with that of *The Bathers* of 1873 (formerly Henri Rouart
Collection).

Former Collection: Gustave Caillebotte, Paris.
Reference: L. Venturi, *Cézanne – son art – son œuvre* (Paris, 1936), vol. 1,
no. 232, p. 116, pl. 63.

62

63

64

VINCENT VAN GOGH, Dutch, 1853–1890
The Postman Roulin
Oil on canvas, 32 × 25½ in.
Gift of Robert Treat Paine, 2nd 35.1892

The postman Étienne Roulin was van Gogh's closest friend in Arles and was the subject of six painted portraits and two drawings. This portrait was probably painted in August 1888. Van Gogh described Roulin in one of his letters: "...a bearded face very like Socrates, a

violent Republican like Tanguy, a man more interesting than most."
The Museum also owns van Gogh's first portrait of Roulin's wife,
La Berceuse, painted in 1889.

Former Collections: C. Hoogendijk, The Hague; Thea Sternheim, Uttwil;
Robert Treat Paine, 2nd, Boston.
References: The Complete Letters of Vincent van Gogh (New York, 1958),
nos. 516–18, 520, 550, 572, 573, 575, 583, B 14; Charles C. Cunningham,
"Roulin the Postman by Vincent van Gogh," MFA *Bulletin* 34, no. 201
(February 1936), pp. 2–3.

65

VINCENT VAN GOGH, Dutch, 1853–1890
The Ravine
Oil on canvas, 28 ³/₄ × 36 ¹/₄ in.
Bequest of Keith McLeod 52.1542

Painted near Saint-Rémy in October 1889, this landscape portrays
the Provençal scenery while a mistral is blowing. After admiring
this painting in the sixth exhibition of the Independents in 1890,
Paul Gauguin wrote to van Gogh: "Among those who work from
nature, you are the only one who thinks.... There is one canvas I
should like to exchange with you for anything of mine you choose.
The one I mean is a mountainous landscape; two very small trav-
elers seem to be climbing in search of the unknown. There is in it
an emotion like Delacroix, with very suggestive colors. Here and
there some red notes, like lights, and the whole in a violet harmony."

Former Collections: Theo van Gogh; Paul Gauguin (?); J. B. Stang, Oslo;
Prince de Wagram, Paris; Keith McLeod, Boston.
References: The Complete Letters of Vincent van Gogh (New York, 1958),
nos. 610, 619, 621–22, B 20; Roger Fry, *Transformations* (New York, 1956),
p. 244; John Rewald, *Post-Impressionism* (New York, 1956), p. 378 (letter
from Gauguin to van Gogh).

65

66

HENRI DE TOULOUSE-LAUTREC, French, 1864–1901
A La Mie
Signed upper right: *T. Lautrec*
Watercolor and gouache on millboard, 21 × 26 3/4 in.
S. A. Denio Fund and General Income for 1940   40.748

Toulouse-Lautrec painted this scene set in the Parisian café, *La Mie*, from a photograph made according to the artist's instructions by his friend, the photographer Paul Sescau, in 1891. Lautrec's friend and traveling companion, Maurice Guibert, and a young professional model posed for it.

Former Collections: Pellet, Paris; Camentron, Paris; D.T.W. Cargill, Glasgow.
References: Gerstle Mack, *Toulouse-Lautrec* (New York, 1938), p. 272 (Sescau photograph, fig. 51); Charles C. Cunningham, "A Famous Toulouse-Lautrec for the Museum," MFA *Bulletin* 39 (April 1941), pp. 27–28.

67

PAUL GAUGUIN, French, 1848–1903
D'où venons-nous? Que sommes-nous? Où allons-nous?
(Where do we come from? What are we? Where are we going?)
Signed and dated upper right: *P Gauguin 1897*
Oil on burlap canvas, 54 ³/₄ × 147 ¹/₂ in.
Arthur Gordon Tompkins Residuary Fund 36.270

Gauguin had decided to commit suicide late in 1897 and painted
this immense canvas in Tahiti as his final testament. He regarded it
as his most important work and lived to discuss it in great detail in
his letters. According to his correspondence, the work should be read
from right to left as a cycle of birth, life, and death. Defending his
approach to symbolism, Gauguin concluded: "Explanatory details
—familiar symbols—would spoil the picture turning it into sad
reality, and the given theme would no longer be a poem."

Former Collections: Ambroise Vollard, Paris; Dr. G. Frizeau, Bordeaux;
Galerie Barbazanges, Paris; J. B. Stang, Oslo; Alfred Gold, Paris; Marie
Harriman Gallery, New York.
References: Charles Morice, *Paul Gauguin* (Paris, 1920), pp. 87, 121, 124
(repr.), 125, 222, 224; J. de Rotonchamp, *Paul Gauguin* (Paris, 1925),
pp. 168–69; James S. Plaut, "A Gauguin Masterpiece," MFA *Bulletin* 34,
no. 203 (June 1936), pp. 33–38; P. Gauguin, *Lettres à sa femme et ses amis*
(Paris, 1946), pp. 288–89, 300, 302; Robert Goldwater, *Paul Gauguin*
(New York, 1957), pp. 140–44; R. Huyghé, R. Field, et. al., *Gauguin* (Paris,
1960), pp. 38, 134, 161–69; Wayne V. Andersen, "Gauguin and a Peruvian
Mummy," *Burlington Magazine* 109 (April 1967), pp. 238–42.

67

68

68

EDVARD MUNCH, Norwegian, 1863–1944
The Voice
Signed lower left: *E. Munch 1893*
Oil on canvas, 34¹/₂ × 42¹/₂ in.
Ernest Wadsworth Longfellow Fund 59.301

The Voice, also called *Summer Night* or *Evening*, was painted in
1893, during Munch's first protracted stay in Berlin. The woman
in *The Voice* is believed to be the artist's close friend and frequent
model, Dagny Juell, later the wife of Stanislas Przybyzewski, a
Polish poet and friend of Munch. A drypoint done in 1895 portrays
the same subject with a few variations.

Former Collection: Mrs. Ragnhild Bäckström, Stockholm.
Reference: Arve Moen, *Edvard Munch, Graphic Art and Paintings*, vol. 2,
Woman and Eros (Oslo, 1957), pp. 18–20.

69

HENRI MATISSE, French, 1869–1954
Carmelina
Signed lower left: *Henri Matisse*
Oil on canvas, 32 × 23¹/₂ in.
Arthur Gordon Tompkins Residuary Fund Res. 32.14

Carmelina, a model, was portrayed in this work of 1903 during the
artist's "dark" period of 1901–04.

Former Collection: Baron S. Fukushima, Paris.
Reference: Alfred H. Barr, Jr., *Matisse: His Art and His Public* (New
York, 1951), pp. 45, 51, 96, 149, 201.

69

70

ODILON REDON, French, 1840–1916
The Large Green Vase
Signed lower left: *Odilon Redon*
Pastel on paper, 29¹/₄ × 24¹/₂ in.
Bequest of John T. Spaulding 48.591

This pastel still life probably dates from about 1910–12, Redon's
most prolific period when flower-pieces were a favorite theme.

Former Collections: Étienne Bignou, Paris; John T. Spaulding, Boston.

71

JOSEPH BLACKBURN, American, active 1752–1774
Isaac Winslow and his Family
Signed and dated lower right: *I. Blackburn Pinx 1755*
Oil on canvas, 54½ × 79½ in.
Abraham Shuman Fund 42.684

Isaac Winslow lived from 1709 to 1777 and graduated from
Harvard in 1727. Mrs. Winslow is seated in the center with baby
Hannah in her lap; daughter Lucy, standing in left profile, holds
branches of fruit.

Former Collections: Samuel Winslow, great-grandson of the sitter, Rox-
bury, Mass., in 1878; Edward M. Winslow, Boston, 1902; George Scott
Winslow, Boston, 1911; Miss Anna W. Winslow, Newcastle, Me., 1942.
References: L. Park, *Blackburn* (Worcester, 1923), no. 88; *American
Paintings in the Museum of Fine Arts, Boston* (Boston, 1969), no. 144, fig.
24.

72

JOHN SINGLETON COPLEY, American, 1738–1815
Paul Revere
Oil on Canvas, 35 × 28½ in.
Gift of Joseph W., William B., and Edward H. R. Revere 30.781

Best known for his participation in the ride to Lexington and Concord on the night of April 19, 1775, Paul Revere was a master silversmith and engraver by trade. It is in this occupation that Copley portrayed him, around 1768–1770, holding a teapot of his own design and manufacture, with engraver's tools on the table before him. The portrait is known to have been in the possession of the sitter's grandson by 1873, and remained in the family until its presentation to the Museum.

Reference: American Paintings in the Museum of Fine Arts, Boston (Boston, 1969), no. 279, fig. 61.

73

JOHN SINGLETON COPLEY, American, 1738–1815
Mrs. Richard Skinner (Dorothy Wendell)
Signed and dated center right: *John Singleton Copley pinx / 1772 / Boston*
Oil on canvas, 39¾ × 30¾ in.
Gift of Mrs. Martin Brimmer 06.2428

The identity of the sitter (1733–1822) has been established by comparison of the features with those in Nathaniel Smibert's portrait of Dorothy Wendell in 1755, and by the similarity of pose and costume to those in Copley's portrait of Dorothy Quincy, Mrs. Skinner's cousin, in 1772.

Former Collections: Lord Lyndhurst, the artist's son, London; Mrs. Martin Brimmer, great-granddaughter of the artist, Boston.
Reference: American Paintings in the Museum of Fine Arts, Boston (Boston, 1969), no. 290, fig. 82.

72

73

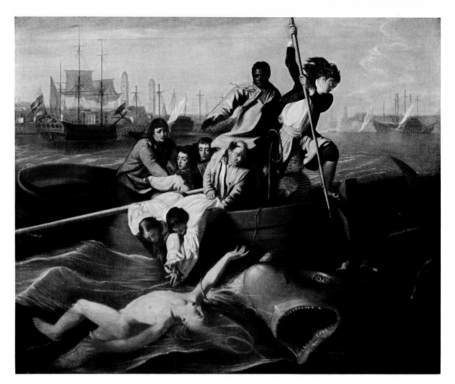

74

74

JOHN SINGLETON COPLEY, American, 1738–1815
Watson and the Shark
Signed and dated inside the stern of the boat: *J. S. Copley P. 1778*
Oil on canvas, 72 × 90¼ in.
Gift of Mrs. George von Lengerke Meyer 89.481

Based on an actual event, *Watson and the Shark* depicts Brook
Watson (1735–1807) as a boy attacked by a shark in Havana harbor. Watson was Lord Mayor of London, 1796–1797. The Boston
painting is a replica, identical in size and similarly signed and dated
1778, of the work exhibited in that year, and later bequeathed to
Christ's Hospital, Surrey, and now in the National Gallery of Art in
Washington. A vertical version signed and dated 1782 is in the collection of the Detroit Institute of Arts. An oil sketch traditionally
ascribed to Copley is in The Metropolitan Museum of Art, and
other studies and drawings are known to exist. A mezzotint of the
composition was made by Valentine Green in 1779.

Former Collection: Lord Lyndhurst, the artist's son, London.
Reference: American Paintings in the Museum of Fine Arts, Boston
(Boston, 1969), no. 299, fig. 73.

75

75

GILBERT STUART, American, 1755–1828
Josiah Quincy
Oil on canvas, 36 × 28 in.
Gift of Eliza Susan Quincy 76.347

Josiah Quincy was mayor of Boston from 1823 to 1828, and president of Harvard from 1829 to 1845. In this portrait of 1824 he is shown against the background of one of his achievements as mayor: the Faneuil Hall Market House, as it was called in his time, more familiar now as the Quincy Market.

Former Collection: Eliza Susan Quincy, daughter of the sitter, Boston, 1824.
References: L. Park, *Gilbert Stuart* (New York, 1926), vol. 2, no. 686, repr. vol 4, p. 419; *American Paintings in the Museum of Fine Arts, Boston* (Boston, 1969), no. 944, fig. 133.

76

JOHN NEAGLE, American, 1796–1860
Pat Lyon at the Forge
Signed and dated lower left: *J. Neagle 1826 & 7*
Oil on canvas, 93 × 68 in.
Deposited by the Boston Athenaeum 16.40

A wash drawing of this composition is still at the Boston Athenaeum. A replica signed and dated 1829 as well as an oil study are in the Pennsylvania Academy of The Fine Arts. Another oil sketch is in the Historical Society of Pennsylvania.

Former Collection: Boston Athenaeum, 1828.
References: R. R. Patrick, "Neagle and Lyon," *Art Bulletin* 33, no. 3 (1951), pp. 187–92, fig. 1; *American Paintings in the Museum of Fine Arts, Boston* (Boston, 1969), no. 777, fig. 171.

76

77

WASHINGTON ALLSTON, American, 1779–1843

Elijah in the Desert

Signed twice on back and dated: *W. Allston 1818* and *W. Allston A.R.A.*

Oil on canvas, 48³/₄ × 72¹/₂ in.

Gift of Mrs. Samuel Hooper and Miss Alice Hooper 70.1

Based on 1 Kings 17: 1–7, *Elijah in the Desert* and *Uriel in the Sun*,
now at Boston University, were painted in 1818 in London for
exhibition at the British Institution. Allston recorded that he painted
the *Elijah* in three weeks, mixing his colors with skim milk. Although
the painting returned with Allston to Boston in 1818 it was later
purchased by Henry Labouchere of London. Eventually it was
brought back to Boston to become the first registered acquisition
of the Museum of Fine Arts.

References: E. P. Richardson, *Allston* (Chicago, 1948), pp. 117, 119–20, 204
(pl. XLII); *American Paintings in the Museum of Fine Arts, Boston*
(Boston, 1969), no. 63, fig. 177.

78

78

HENRY F. DARBY, American, 1829–1897
The Rev. John Atwood and his Family
Signed and dated lower right: *H.F. DARBY Painter/1845.*
Oil on canvas, 72 × 96 ¼ in.
M. and M. Karolik Collection 62.269

Darby painted this picture in 1845, when he was sixteen years old.
He refers to it in his diary, which is also in the possession of the
Boston Museum. Atwood, a resident of Concord, New Hampshire,
was nominated for governor in 1850, but bolted the Democratic
party because of its pro-slavery policy.

Former Collections: Rev. John Atwood, Concord and New Boston, N.H.;
Solomon Dodge Atwood, his son, New Boston, 1873; Florence and Annie
Atwood, his daughters, New Boston, 1915.
References: Darby's manuscript diary, 1894, p. 41; *American Paintings in
the Museum of Fine Arts, Boston* (Boston, 1969), no. 321, p. 256.

79

FITZ HUGH LANE, American, 1804–1865
Boston Harbor
Oil on canvas, 26 ¼ × 42 in.
M. and M. Karolik Collection by exchange and gift of John
Wilmerding 66.339

Lane was a native of Gloucester who specialized in marine views.
Several versions of this work of around 1850–55 are known to exist.
An earlier view of Boston harbor, painted in 1845, is in the White
House in Washington.

Former Collections: Probably Mrs. Charles M. Pierce (about 1840–1922),
New Bedford, Mass.; Mrs. Willis E. Lougee, New Bedford; Mrs. Grace
H. Sargent, New Bedford; Mrs. Thomas W. Farnsworth, Jr., New Bedford,
about 1960.
Reference: *American Paintings in the Museum of Fine Arts, Boston*
(Boston, 1969), no. 712, fig. 263.

79

80

GEORGE CALEB BINGHAM, American, 1811–1879
The Squatters
Signed and dated lower left: *G Bingham 1850.*
Oil on canvas, 23 × 28 in.
Promised Gift of Henry L. Shattuck

In a letter dated November 18, 1850, the same year in which he painted *The Squatters,* Bingham wrote about the painting to the American Art Union, the group to which he sold it. Sketches for the old man and the young man represented in the painting are nos. 96 and 44, respectively, in Bingham's sketchbook, now in the St. Louis Mercantile Library.

Former Collections: N. P. Hood, 1852; Henry L. Shattuck, Brookline, Mass., 1937.
Reference: American Paintings in the Museum of Fine Arts, Boston (Boston, 1969), no. 131, fig. 285.

81

MARTIN JOHNSON HEADE, American, 1819–1904
Approaching Storm: Beach near Newport
Oil on canvas, 28 × 58 1/4 in.
M. and M. Karolik Collection 45.889

This picture, painted in the 1860's, was relined before coming to the Museum, and it is said that an inscription that placed the scene on Naragansett Bay with a thunderstorm approaching was covered in the process.

Former Collections: Henry Goddard Pickering, Boston, 1926; Mrs. Richard Y. Fitz Gerald, Boston.
References: M. and M. Karolik Collection of American Paintings, 1815 to 1865 (Cambridge, 1949), no. 137 (repr.); *American Paintings in the Museum of Fine Arts, Boston* (Boston, 1969), no. 511, fig. 329.

80

81

82

82

JOHN SINGER SARGENT, American, 1856–1925
The Daughters of Edward Darley Boit
Signed and dated lower right: *John S. Sargent. 1882*
Oil on canvas, 87 × 87 in.
Gift of Mary Louisa Boit, Florence D. Boit, Jane Hubbard Boit, and
Julia Overing Boit, in Memory of their Father 19.124

From left to right are Mary, born 1874, Florence, born 1868, Jane,
born 1870, and Julia, born 1878. Edward Boit of Boston was a
painter and a close friend of Sargent. The children are portrayed in
the drawing room of the Boit's Paris residence.

Former Collection: Edward Darley Boit, Paris, 1882.
References: David McKibben, *Sargent's Boston* (Boston, 1956), pp. 29–33,
85, fig. 14; *American Paintings in the Museum of Fine Arts, Boston*
(Boston, 1969), no. 858, fig. 454.

83

WINSLOW HOMER, American, 1836–1910
The Lookout — "All's Well"
Signed and dated lower right: *Homer / 1896*
Oil on canvas, 40 × 30¹/₄ in.
William Wilkins Warren Fund 99.23

Painted at Prout's Neck, Maine, where Homer lived. The Cooper-
Hewitt Museum in New York owns several drawings and studies
for the picture. W. H. W. Bicknell did an etching of the composition.

Former Collections: At Doll and Richards, Boston, 1897; Thomas
B. Clarke Collection Sale, American Art Association, New York, 1899.
References: L. Goodrich, *Homer* (New York, 1959), pl. 77; A. Ten Eyck
Gardner, *Homer* (New York, 1969), p. 214; *American Paintings in the
Museum of Fine Arts, Boston* (Boston, 1969), no. 566, fig. 440.

83

84

WINSLOW HOMER, American, 1836–1910
Long Branch, New Jersey
Signed and dated lower right: *Winslow Homer / 1869.*
Oil on canvas, 16 × 21³/₄ in.
Charles Henry Hayden Fund 41.631

The same subject appears in several of Homer's woodcuts.

Former Collections: Robert Vonnoh, Philadelphia, before 1906; Sherrill
Babcock, New York.
References: L. Goodrich, *Homer* (New York, 1959), pl. 24; *American
Paintings in the Museum of Fine Arts, Boston* (Boston, 1969), no. 560, fig.
436.

85

85

THOMAS EAKINS, American, 1844–1916
Starting out after Rail
Signed and dated on stern of boat: *Eakins 74.*, and lower left: *Eakins*.
Oil on canvas, 24 × 20 in.
Charles Henry Hayden Fund 35.1953

The figures in this painting of 1874 have been identified from a
watercolor of the same year entitled *Harry Young, of Moyamensing,
and Sam Helhower, "The Pusher", Going Rail Shooting*. Both were
friends of Eakins. Moyamensing is part of the Philadelphia marsh-
lands on the Delaware River. The watercolor version was shown in
the seventh annual exhibition of the American Society of Painters
in Watercolors, New York. A horizontal version in oil, less brilliant
in color, entitled *Sailing* is in the Philadelphia Museum of Art.

Former Collection: Purchased from the artist in 1915 by Janet Walker,
Philadelphia.
Reference: American Paintings in the Museum of Fine Arts, Boston
(Boston, 1969), no. 376, fig. 441.

86

MARY CASSATT, American, 1844–1926
At the Opera
Oil on canvas, 31$^{1}/_{2}$ × 25$^{1}/_{2}$ in.
Charles Henry Hayden Fund 10.35

At the Opera is reproduced in an article reviewing the second exhibition of the Society of American Artists held in New York 1879,
but is not included in the catalogue. This painting is related to other
works of the artist: notably *In the Box*, painted around 1879
(private collection), and *The Loge*, of around 1882 (Chester Dale
Collection, National Gallery of Art, Washington).

Former Collection: J. Gardner Cassatt, brother of the artist, 1880.
References: W. C. Brownell, "The Younger Painters of America, III,"
Scribners' Monthly 23, no. 3 (1881), p. 333 (engraving by A. F. P. Davis,
1880); *American Paintings in the Museum of Fine Arts, Boston* (Boston,
1969), no. 196, fig. 473.

86

87

WILLIAM MICHAEL HARNETT, American, 1848–1892
Old Models
Signed and dated lower left: *W M Harnett / 1892* (initials in monogram)
Oil on canvas, 54 × 28 in.
Charles Henry Hayden Fund 39.761

Old Models, variously titled *My Models, The Old Cupboard,* and *The Old Cupboard Door,* is said to have been Harnett's last work. In the catalogue of the sale of his estate (Thomas Birche's Sons, Philadelphia, 1893, no. 27) it is stated that the painting was made for the Chicago World's Columbian Exposition of 1893, but Harnett died in the meantime and it was not shown.

Former Collection: William J. Hughes, Washington.
Reference: American Paintings in the Museum of Fine Arts, Boston (Boston, 1969), no. 488, fig. 449.

88

JOHN FREDERICK PETO, American, 1854–1907
The Poor Man's Store
Signed and dated upper left: *J. F. Peto / —85*
Oil on canvas and wood, 36 × 25½ in.
M. and M. Karolik Collection 62.278

Five years before this painting was finished another with a similar title was exhibited in the annual exhibition of the Pennsylvania Academy of Fine Arts in Philadelphia.

Reference: American Paintings in the Museum of Fine Arts, Boston (Boston, 1969), no. 810, fig. 448.

87

88

89

CHILDE HASSAM, American, 1859–1935
Grand Prix Day
Signed and dated lower left: *Childe Hassam Paris—1887.*
Oil on canvas, 24 × 34 in.
Ernest Wadsworth Longfellow Fund 64.983

A larger, somewhat more finished version entitled *Le Grand Prix,*
signed in the same way but undated, is in the New Britain Museum
of Art, Connecticut.

Reference: American Paintings in the Museum of Fine Arts, Boston
(Boston, 1969), no. 498, fig. 518.

90

MARSDEN HARTLEY, American, 1877–1943
Carnival of Autumn
Oil on canvas, 30¹/4 × 30¹/8 in.
Charles Henry Hayden Fund 68.296

Painted in 1908, *Carnival of Autumn* is an early, American example
of the reaction against Impressionism in which the Symbolist
precepts of arbitrary color and stylized form producing a strong
decorative style are expressed. Symbolist influence is also reflected
in the title, in which the "idea" rather than the fact of the picture is
phrased. Here, as in much of Hartley's late work, the landscape of
Maine is the inspiration.

Former Collection: Ione and Hudson Walker.
Reference: Elizabeth McCausland, *Marsden Hartley* (Minneapolis, 1952),
pp. 13–14.

91

91

MAURICE PRENDERGAST, American, 1859–1924
Eight Bathers
Signed lower center: *Prendergast*
Oil on canvas, 28¼ × 24 in.
Abraham Shuman Fund 61.663

Only in the last decade of his life did Prendergast leave Boston for
New York, and even then he continued to spend his summers on
the New England coast. On his return to his New York studio, he
would rework watercolor impressions of the summer into oils
such as *Eight Bathers* (1916–1918). The frame was designed by the
artist's brother Charles.

Former Collection: Mrs. Charles Prendergast, Westport, Conn.
References: Hedley Howell Rhys, *Maurice Prendergast, 1859–1924*
(Cambridge, 1960), pp. 52, 54, no. 38; *American Paintings in the Museum
of Fine Arts, Boston* (Boston, 1969), no. 818, fig. 536.

92

GEORGE LUKS, American, 1867–1933
Bulfinch Houses, Beacon Hill
Signed lower right: *George Luks*
Oil on canvas, 36¼ × 30¼ in.
Emily L. Ainsley Fund 60.538

Beacon Hill is typified by these bow-front town houses in the style
of Boston's great architect of the Federal Period, Charles Bulfinch.
George Luks painted several of these cityscapes while visiting
Boston in the summer of 1923.

Former Collection: Mr. and Mrs. Quincy Adams Shaw McKean, Boston.
Reference: American Paintings in the Museum of Fine Arts, Boston*
(Boston, 1969), no. 734, fig. 546.

92

93

GEORGE BELLOWS, American, 1882–1925
Emma and Her Children
Oil on canvas, 59 × 65 in.
Gift of Subscribers and the John Lowell Gardner Fund 25.105

From 1920 to 1924 Bellows spent his summers in Woodstock,
New York. This group portrait of his wife and daughters was
painted in the studio there in September 1923.

Former Collection: Mrs. George Bellows.
References: Marian King, *A Gallery of Mothers and their Children*
(Philadelphia and New York, 1958), pp. 50–51; *American Paintings in the
Museum of Fine Arts, Boston* (Boston, 1969), no. 92, fig. 553.

94

94

LYONEL FEININGER, American, 1871–1956
Regler Church, Erfurt
Signed upper left: *Feininger*
Oil on canvas, 50 × 40¼ in.
Charles Henry Hayden Fund 57.198

Erfurt is a town near Weimar that was popular with the Bauhaus group because of its many churches. Feininger painted the Reglerkirche, a church of Augustinian canons named for an Erfurt family, in 1930 while he was on the faculty of the Bauhaus in Dessau.

Former Collections: Magistrate of Dessau; Anhaltisches Landesmuseum, Dessau; G. David Thompson, Pittsburgh.
Reference: American Paintings in the Museum of Fine Arts, Boston (Boston, 1969), no. 394, fig. 583.

95

EDWARD HOPPER, American, 1882–1967
Room in Brooklyn
Signed lower right: *Edward Hopper*
Oil on canvas, 29 × 34 in.
Charles Henry Hayden Fund 35.66

In a letter of March 21, 1935, the artist stated: "There is not a great deal to be said about the painting of the 'Room in Brooklyn.' It was largely improvised, and was painted in 1932."

Former Collection: Purchased from the artist.
Reference: American Paintings in the Museum of Fine Arts, Boston (Boston, 1969), no. 373, fig. 558.

95

96

PABLO PICASSO, Spanish, born 1881
Standing Figure
Signed on reverse at upper right: *Picasso*
Oil on canvas, 59 × 39¹/₂ in.
Juliana Cheney Edwards Collection 58.796

Painted in the winter of 1908 in Paris, *Standing Figure* (also known as *Femme aux bras levés*) is a study for the central figure in *Three Women* in the Hermitage, Leningrad.

Former Collections: Daniel-Henry Kahnweiler, Paris; Dr. Fritz Nathan, Zurich.
Reference: C. Zervos, *Pablo Picasso, œuvres de 1906 à 1912* (Paris, 1942), vol. 2, no. 107, p. 50, repr.

97

PABLO PICASSO, Spanish, born 1881
Rape of the Sabines
Signed upper right: *Picasso;* working dates on reverse, from January 9 to February 7, 1963
Oil on canvas, 77 × 51¹/₄ in.
Robert J. Edwards Fund (Juliana Cheney Edwards Collection), Fanny P. Mason Fund and Arthur Gordon Tompkins Residuary Fund 64.709

Picasso's subject matter is derived from the Rome of Romulus and Remus by way of Jacques-Louis David's neoclassical composition of 1799. Painted at Mougins in 1963, the *Rape of the Sabines* is a timely reiteration of Picasso's *Guernica* of 1937.

Reference: Carlton Lake, "Picasso," *Boston Magazine 57,* no. 3 (March 1965), pp. 33–35.

96

97

98

NICOLAS DE STAËL, French, 1914–1955
Rue Gauguet
Signed lower left: *Staël;* signed and dated on reverse: *Nicolas de Staël 1949*
Oil on panel, 78¹/₂ × 94³/₄ in.
Arthur Gordon Tompkins Residuary Fund 57.385

The painting was finished in 1949 after about two years' work in the artist's studio in the Rue Gauguet, Paris.

Former Collection: Theodore Schempp, Paris.

99

LEE GATCH, American, born 1902
Gothic Night
Signed lower right: *L Gatch*
Oil on canvas, 42¹/₄ × 46¹/₄ in.
Charles Henry Hayden Fund 57.666

The artist wrote of this painting of 1957 in a letter to the Museum
later in the same year:

"While I have long been moved by that period of History intensely
religious and profoundly intellectual referred to by some authors as
the Gothic Night, I would rather lay claim that my inspiration was
more the result of direct visual experience.... It was through the
struggle for a finer subjectivity that *Gothic Night* finally emerged—
came to the surface, so to speak....

In my youth I was a hunter and the night forest fascinated me, especially the great arches made by the trees against the brilliant November sky. This was the visual experience that was to find spiritual discipline many years later."

References: Martica Sawin, "The Paintings of Lee Gatch," *Arts* 32 (May 1958), pp. 30–33; Barbara Guest, "Avery and Gatch: Lonely Americans," *Art News* 59 (March 1960), pp. 42–45; Perry T. Rathbone, *Lee Gatch* (New York, 1960), pp. 12–13, 19–20; Allen Stuart Weller, *Art U.S.A. Now* (New York, 1963), p. 112.

100

FRANZ KLINE, American, 1910–1962
Probst I
Signed and dated on reverse at center: *Franz Kline — 60*
Oil on canvas, 108 × 79⅝ in.
Promised Gift of Susan Morse Hilles

The title of this composition is believed to refer to the painter Jack Probst, a friend of the artist. It appears that Kline never intended the painting for Probst but simply used his name for the title because he liked the sound of it.

Former Collection: Susan Morse Hilles, New Haven, Conn.

100

Index of Artists

References are to catalogue
numbers not pages.